W9-CJA-037

The Power of the Precious Blood

**A Bible Study on
The Blood of Jesus Christ
by
Gwen R. Shaw**

**End-Time Handmaidens, Inc.
Engeltal
P.O. Box 447
Jasper, Ark. 72641**

Printed in the United States of America

FOREWORD

The time has come when the message of the Lord's heart to the church is that His Bride must come into a deeper understanding of what it means to do WARFARE using the Shield of FAITH, on which is inscribed the SEAL and COAT OF ARMS of Glory. . . THE BLOOD of Jesus Christ, our HIGH Priest. We have 'Pled the Blood' for years, but with the coward's voice, as though we were begging Satan to leave us alone, because, after all, we were people of the Blood. It is true, Satan has sucked the blood of saints ever since Abel was slain by Cain. But it is not our blood we need to protect. The BLOOD OF JESUS CHRIST NEEDS NO PROTECTION EITHER. INSTEAD IT IS THE PROOF THAT JESUS WAS THE VICTOR AND THE CHURCH NEEDS TO LEARN HOW TO RAISE THAT BANNER HIGH, FOR IT VALIDATES THE NEW COVENANT AND THE ONE WHO MADE IT. . . OUR LORD AND KING. The message of the Atonement has been set aside in the flurry over Praise, Worship. It needs re-emphasis from the standpoint of SPIRITUAL WARFARE.

—Betty Platt

INTRODUCTION

It is with much fear and trembling that I begin this Bible study on the Power of the Precious Blood. I feel so unworthy to even try to approach this great and precious truth. I realize that we are TOUCHING HEAVENLY THINGS when we in any way minister on that which concerns the shedding of blood.

And yet I know that without the power of the Blood of Jesus and what it has done in my life, I would be an utterly lost and hopeless sinner with no hope for eternity. It is with His Blood Jesus has brought me nigh to God, cleansed me, redeemed me, sanctified me and reconciled me to God.

It is thirty years since I arrived as a young woman in Shanghai, China on my first mission field. I had no experience as a minister or missionary; I had very little knowledge of the language (only what I could acquire in one year of the study of Chinese at the University of Toronto); I was without a mission board behind me—no promised support and very little talent but I took with me the knowledge of the power of the Blood of Jesus, a truth that had been made real to me through a little old saint in Canada who had taken me under her wings and shared this truth of God with me.

In these thirty years I have learned many things and had many new truths revealed to me, but the "old, old story" of the power of the Precious Blood of Jesus is the greatest of them all. And now by God's command and through His help I open my only textbook that I intend to use to teach you— THE HOLY BIBLE—and I begin to share with you the immutability of the efficaciousness and power of the Precious Blood of Jesus.

—Sister Gwen

CHAPTER 1

My Experience of Victory Through the Blood

Let me begin by telling you one of the great experiences of my life.

I was living in Hong Kong with my three small sons when one Sunday morning I was awakened from a terrible dream that left me trembling.

In the dream I had been approached by Satan. He was so full of evil and there issued from him such darkness that I was repulsed by his presence. He looked at me with a cunning sneer and said mockingly, "I have power to harm you." I immediately sensed that he was challenging me to go to war with him. I knew, too, that I didn't want to do this. I answered, "I know you have power to do me much harm. But you are afraid of the BLOOD."

Immediately he answered me, "I'm not afraid of the blood of bulls and goats."

For a desperate moment I didn't know what to say; then the Lord prompted me, "No, but you are afraid of the Blood of Jesus."

Immediately when I said that he began to shake and tremble. With great shaking he said, "Yes, of that I am afraid." And right in front of my eyes he began to shrivel up and get smaller and smaller.

I awakened just frozen with fear. I knew that Satan was going to attack me, but that God had given me the one great key for deliverance. And I would have to use THAT key—the Power of the Precious Blood of Jesus.

I got out of bed and dropped on my knees. I began to pray and call on God to give me the strength to go through the battle that I was positive lay just ahead of me.

About two hours later, one of Hong Kong's most

1

anointed missionary sisters visited me. I was surprised at her coming so early in the morning. She told me that God had told her to come.

So I shared my dream with her. When she had finished hearing it, she said, "Sister Gwen, you will be attacked by Satan in a very powerful way, but when it happens, remember God has given you the key. Plead the Blood of Jesus and God will give you the victory." I knew this was a confirmation from God. I thanked her and after praying with me she left.

Two hours later I left my boys in the care of a Chinese woman and went out to the country to preach. All day long I thought about the dream God had given to me and I wondered just how Satan would attack me. I had to go to two meetings to preach. When I returned from the second service back to the city and stepped in the door of my home, the Chinese woman met me with the words, "Tommy is sick."

Tommy was my youngest. He was just six years old. I immediately knew that my battle had begun. Rushing into the bedroom where he lay, flushed with a high fever, I was told that almost from the time I had left home he had been sick. I took his temperature. It was very high. I knelt by his bed and prayed for him and began immediately to plead the Blood of Jesus over my child.

All that night he slept with me, groaning with the fever and misery he was feeling. I laid my hand on him and pleaded for Jesus to cover him with His Blood.

Tuesday he was no better, nor Wednesday. The fever seemed to only go higher and higher. All the time I pled the Blood of Jesus. On Thursday his temperature was down, but when he got out of bed, he walked all bent over and crooked. It seemed as if he had become deformed.

Immediately the thought "meningitis" came to me. Satan whispered to me, "See, I've given him meningitis and neither you nor your 'pleading the blood' could help anything."

On Friday a Chinese sister visited me. When she saw how sick Tommy was, she immediately got on her knees and with tears began to pray. "Lord," she cried, "I am a mother and I have children. I know how this mother's heart is broken to see her son so sick. I beseech Thee, heal Tommy. When he wakes up tomorrow morning, let him be well."

Suddenly I knew we had the victory. I began to rejoice even though there was no sign of healing.

The next morning when he woke up, he jumped out of bed and came running over to me straight and strong as ever. I raised my hands in praises to God. The Blood of Jesus had won the victory.

I will never forget those many days and nights of struggling against Satan, claiming the Blood of Jesus as my only hope for my child's deliverance. Sometimes I had almost given up. But God had given the victory. He had delivered Tommy out of the power of Satan through the power of the precious Blood of Jesus.

Why Plead the Blood?

So many times we hear the words, "Plead the blood." And sometimes we wonder what it means. Let me explain it like this:

When one is accused of a crime, the accused one has the right to argue his case before the court of law on a basis of "guilty" or "not guilty." The presentation with which the accused faces his charges can make all the difference in the results.

Before God we ALL stand as condemned sinners. We are guilty of every vice in the book—hatred, anger, jealousy, unforgiveness, and many more. We are challenged to enter our plea, to defend ourselves against our accuser. We cannot ignore it; we know we are guilty so we can't plead "not guilty." We must only be honest with ourselves. And so, we plead our case before the Judge, in the only way that we can

3

find mercy: that is, through the Blood of Jesus. The Blood of Jesus is our defense. It is our witness. It was poured out for us from the riven side of Emmanuel and He promised in His Word it would wash away all our guilty stains. Thank God that God, the Judge, is PLEASED to SEE US THROUGH THE BLOOD OF HIS SON.

So we enter our plea: Not through any good works that we have done, but only because of the Blood of HIS SON.

The Blood is our plea.

The Blood is our covering.

The Blood is the price that was paid for our redemption.

The Blood is our witness.

The Blood "speaketh better things than that of Abel" (Heb. 12:24).

The Blood speaks of life and forgiveness,
mercy and cleansing,
and of power to deliver us from the
sentence of death.

As a sinner I plead the Blood of Jesus for my sins.

As a Christian I plead the Blood for my failures and weaknesses.

As a warrior against evil, I plead it as my protection against the attack of Satan. For this I know: Satan is afraid of the power of the Blood of Jesus.

4

STUDY QUESTIONS

1. Read Hebrews, chapters 1 and 2.

2. Memorize Hebrews 12:24.

3. What does it mean to "plead the Blood?"

4. Why is Satan so evil?

5. What does Satan fear most of all?

6. In what way have even the most right-living people sinned?

7. How do I receive mercy from God?

8. After I am saved, do I still need the Blood of Jesus?

CHAPTER 2

The Spirit of Cain

The first record we have of human blood being shed is when Cain slew his brother Abel. Cain was the first of all mankind ever to be born. When Eve gave birth to him she said, "I've gotten a man from the Lord." However, it seems that there was a lot of sin in Cain. He was full of anger and jealousy toward his brother. He was cruel and cunning. When he brought his offering to God, God did not accept it. "But unto Cain and to his offering he had not respect" (Genesis 4:5). Instead of humbling himself, searching his heart and asking forgiveness, Cain was very angry and his countenance fell. What a terrible thing it is to see one go about with a fallen countenance—an angry expression!

God spoke to him. God tried to intercept him before he could destroy himself. "And the Lord said unto Cain, Why art thou wroth? And why is thy countenance fallen? If thou doest right, shalt thou not be accepted? And if thou doest not right, sin croucheth at the door and waits to conquer you. But you should rule over it" (Genesis 4:6, 7, The Holy Bible in Modern English).

God does not want that sin should rule over us and be king of our lives. "Let not sin therefore reign in your mortal body" (Romans 6:12). In Chinese it reads, "Do not allow sin to be king of your perishable body."

God could not accept Cain's offering because he came to God without forgiving his brother. Jesus said, "If thou bring thy gift to the altar, and there rememberest that thy brother hath ought against thee; leave there thy gift before the altar, and go thy way; first be reconciled to thy brother, and then come and offer thy gift" (Matthew 5:23, 24). Another

6

translation reads, "Therefore, even if you have carried your offering up to the altar, and you should there discover that your brother has suffered any wrong by you, leave your offering even before the altar, and go away; first be reconciled to your brother, and then returning, present your offering." It is no avail to bring our many sacrifices and great works to God if we are causing grief and heartaches to another of His children. The suffering which we carelessly inflict upon God's children by our sinful ways of criticism and jealousy and covetousness is far greater than we have ever realized. Is it any wonder that God cannot hear us when we pray and call upon Him when our gifts are wrapped in anger and be-ribboned with unforgiveness!

It was this spirit of the evil one that took over Cain and caused him to kill his brother. When God asked Cain, "Where is Abel, thy brother?" He answered, "I know not: am I my brother's keeper?" The word "keeper" comes from the Hebrew SHAMAR (shawmar), to hedge about, to guard, protect.

This is the spirit of Cain today. Sad to say, there are many Cainites in the Christian family of God.

The Blood of Abel

It was then that God spoke some of the most confounding truths ever spoken, and still not understood fully by the greatest Bible scholars today.

"What hast thou done? The voice of thy brother's blood crieth unto me from the ground" (Genesis 4:10).

The word *voice* comes from the Hebrew QOL (kole), to call aloud, to cry. What was it that God sensed from the spilled-out blood of Abel? We know that all sound is vibration. We hear through invisible vibrations which fill the air. But there are different degrees of vibrations which the ear cannot pick up. The human ear cannot even hear some of the vibrations of sound that a dog's ear can hear. And then there are some that even the dog can't hear. What cry was

7

God hearing? He was feeling in His infinite being of love, the vibrations of hurt and sorrow and pain from the warm blood of the persecuted brother.

God said, "And now art thou cursed from the earth, which hath opened her mouth to receive thy brother's blood from thy hand" (Genesis 4:11).

Again, strange to understand and mysterious words! God is telling Cain that the earth loved the one he hated. The earth received the one he rejected. The very dust out of which Abel was created received Abel back to itself. The earth "opened its mouth" to receive the suffering, persecuted one's blood. And in this great act of love which the earth performed—by receiving the persecuted one—a curse from the earth fell on the persecutor.

By your gentle acts of love and kindness, you bring comfort to the despised and rejected ones. And in so doing, you also cause a curse to fall on the oppressor. You do not need to fight the Cainite to bring him into judgment; you only need to love the ones he hates. That is already his judgment.

Love Makes Us Our Brother's Keeper

When we bring Bibles to the persecuted Christians who are suffering from their own people behind the iron curtain, we are doing the greatest act of love that mortal man is capable of doing. We are "opening our mouths" to receive our brother's blood—to share in his suffering. "Partly, because ye were made a gazingstock both by reproaches and afflictions; and partly, because ye became companions of them that were so used" [or so treated] (Hebrews 10:33).

Wherever the blood of Abel was spilled on the earth, the earth turned red, taking on it the crimson of its flow. You cannot help the sufferer without being identified with him. And in helping him you will bring judgment on his enemies.

8

Learning the Worth of the Blood

God knew the worth of the blood, but man had yet to learn its preciousness. God would teach it to them. It would take 4,000 years, the death of many humans, the slaughter of many animals in sacrifice, and finally the poured-out Blood of His Son. But they would learn it in such a way that finally at the end John heard them singing praises to Him Who by His Blood had redeemed them to God out of every kindred, tongue, people, and nation (Revelation 5:9).

STUDY QUESTIONS

1. Read Hebrews, chapter 3, and Genesis, Chapters 1-4.

2. Memorize Romans 6:12.

3. What was the difference between Cain and Abel's offerings?

4. Why did Cain kill Abel?

5. Why could God not accept Cain's offering?

6. In what way did Abel's voice speak?

7. How can you be your brother's keeper?

8. How can you bring judgment on him that is evil?

CHAPTER 3

The Adamic Covenant

From the time of the fall, it seems to have been necessary for blood to be shed for the sealing of each new covenant God has made with man.

The antediluvian dispensation (which is timed from the fall to the flood) began with God making a covering of skins for Adam and Eve. While there is a possibility that that covering of skin is the one we wear today, it is also highly probable that God used the skin of an animal to cover the nakedness of Adam and Eve.

"Unto Adam also and to his wife did the Lord God make coats of skins, and clothed them" (Genesis 3:21).

The word "skins" in Hebrew is OWR, skin, by implication hide, leather. "Clothed" in Hebrew is LABASH, to wrap around, put on a garment, to clothe oneself or another, to arm, to put on, to wear.

Nowhere is it stated in the Bible that God slew an animal to clothe Adam and Eve, but it seems highly probable that He did this. In so doing, He clothed the nakedness of man with the sacrifice of a living creature.

It is probably from this example that Abel learned to bring to God an offering of the firstlings of his flock (the best and fattest of his sheep).

Man has always felt his nakedness before God and has sought to be "covered." Abel, righteous man that he was, knew that his covering was not his father Adam, or his own skin, or the garments he wore, but the covering which the shed blood of a sacrifice alone can give.

So it is today. Our only "covering" as we approach the dazzling brilliance of a just and holy God is not another mortal man of the same cursed flesh as our own, but the Blood of the slain Lamb of God. As we are covered by His blood we can approach the Almighty and have audience with our God. Yes, we may see God *and Live!*

Noahic Covenant

The second covenant that God made with man—Noahic —was also sealed with blood. The very hour that Noah went out of the ark he built an altar unto the Lord and took of every clean beast and every clean fowl, and offered burnt offerings on the altar. And God smelled a sweet savour (a pleasant, sweet perfume); and the Lord said in His heart, "I will never again curse the ground for man's sake (to the labor of man) although the imagination of man's heart is evil from his youth; and never again will I smite every living thing, as I have done. During the whole existence of the earth, sowing and harvest, cold and heat, summer and winter, day and night shall not cease" (Genesis 8:21-22). Then God blessed Noah and commanded him to multiply and promised to supply him with food from the beast of the field and the vegetation of the earth. And then God made a covenant concerning blood.

"But flesh with the life thereof, which is the blood thereof, shall ye not eat" (Genesis 9:4). Another translation renders it, "But the flesh with its life, its blood, you shall not eat." God said if man would eat the flesh of an animal which had not been properly slaughtered first, whose blood had not been shed, he would take that man's life from him.

To us who always slaughter an animal before we eat it, this law seems superficial. But there are countries where man eats living animals, even living humans. This is true of the Satanists even in our country who cut off the fingers of their sacrificial victims and chew on them, and drink their blood, besides doing many other damnable and cursed things which we have no desire to go into now.

God was teaching Noah to honor the blood of beast and

11

of man, because He said there was life in the blood. On the battlefield many perfectly healthy humans, strong and young, can get only a small cut in one of his main arteries or veins, and you'll see his life flow out with every drop of blood that pours from that small and non-infected wound. No germ killed him, no deadly disease, there was no mangling of limb, just the loss of his blood was the loss of his life.

God said, "Whoso sheddeth man's blood, by man shall his blood be shed: for in the image of God made he man" (Genesis 9:6).

The Abrahamic Covenant

God made a covenant with Abraham (Genesis 12:1-5). A covenant of righteousness by faith. This did not eliminate Abraham from making offerings to God. He built many altars to God (Genesis 12:7-8, 13:18, 22:9).

In Genesis 15:9 we read of God asking him to bring a particular offering. "Offer me an heifer of three years old, a she goat of three years old, a ram of three years, a turtledove and a young pigeon . . ." When he obeyed God, God gave him a revelation of what would happen in the next four generations of his descendants.

The last altar that Abraham built was when he was ready to offer up his son Isaac (Genesis 22:9). After that we never read about him building another altar or offering another sacrifice. It was not necessary. His love had been tested to its limit and he had not been found wanting.

God did not require the blood of Isaac for an offering because God would need only ONE, that was His only begotten Son, to die for the sins of the world and Abraham. And until He would come and be that offering, God would accept only the blood of animals. When men in heathen rites offered up their children in the sacrifice fires of demon worship, it was an abomination to God.

STUDY QUESTIONS

1. Read Hebrews, chapters 4 and 5.

2. Memorize Hebrews 13:20-21.

3. How did God cover Adam and Eve?
   Do you think He killed an animal?

4. What is our true covering?

5. Describe the Noahic covenant.

6. What law did God give Noah that still stands today?

7. In what way was the Abrahamic covenant different from the Noahic?

8.. Why did God not require the death of Isaac?

CHAPTER 4

The Mosaic Covenant

The greatest deliverance, the most tremendous emancipation mankind had ever known up until that time was brought about through the death of a lamb for a household. For 430 years Abraham's children had dwelt in Egypt. Much of this time they were the most wretched of slaves, living in poverty and fear. Their infant sons were torn from the mothers' arms and slain by the cruel oppressors. God had heard their cry. He remembered his covenant with Abraham: "But in the fourth generation they shall come hither again" (Genesis 15:16). It was exactly four generations from the time Israel went to Egypt that she came back out. JACOB went in with his sons and grandchildren, LEVI, KOHATH, AMRAM, AARON (I Chronicles 6:1-3). It was Aaron's generation that came out. God's word is true. It's forever settled in heaven.

And then God spoke to Moses, the brother of Aaron, and commanded him to bring out his people.

Nine different, terrible plagues struck the land of Egypt from the hand of an angry God. Still Pharaoh would not let the people go. Then came the warning of a tenth and final one, a plague so awful that it would touch every family in Egypt.

The Passover Night

"Thus saith the Lord, about midnight I will go out into the midst of Egypt and all the firstborn in the land of Egypt shall die, from the firstborn of Pharaoh that sitteth upon his throne, even unto the firstborn of the maid-servant that is behind the mill, and all the firstborn of the beast.

"And there shall be a great cry throughout all the land of Egypt, such as there was none like it, nor shall be like it any more" (Exodus 11:4-6). On that dreadful day God himself was sending out the destroyer to work a work of judgment in the land of Egypt. But God said He would spare Israel so that all may know that the Lord doth put a difference between the Egyptians and Israel.

The Slain Lamb

What was this difference? It was the token of the blood. God told Israel through Moses that on the tenth day of the month they should select a male lamb of the first year, separate it from the other sheep and goats. On the eve of the fourth day it was to be killed before witnesses and the BLOOD of the slain lamb painted on the two sides and the lintel of the doors of their homes. They were to gather together and eat all of the lamb in a state of readiness, for their deliverance would come instantaneously.

God said He would pass through the land at midnight to execute judgment. And then He said, "And the blood shall be to you for a token upon the houses where you are; and when I see the blood I will pass over you, and I will not allow the destroyer to come into your houses to smite you" (Exodus 12:23).

The Destroyer Destroys

He promised the children of Israel that the blood of the innocent lamb would be their protection from all danger, death, or injury. But they must stay inside the house. "None of you shall go out at the door of his house until the morning" (Exodus 12:22). What a night of terror that was as the destroyer silently passed from house to house! In every home a firstborn was suddenly found dead. The father in

15

one place, and perhaps his oldest son. In another it was a mother, a daughter, an aunt or an uncle, first and second cousins. The death angel slipped quietly, quickly from prison to farmhouse, from cottage to palace, from merchant to soldier, from one end of Egypt to another. The night of judgment had come—and there was no defense. None could save his life. No doctor could help, no medicine could lessen the danger or the terror. There was only one means of salvation: that was the dark red markings of the blood of the slain lamb upon the door of the house. As the destroyer passed through the streets, the Lord was traveling with him as judge of Egypt and saviour of Israel. When He saw the blood on the door, He would not allow the destroyer to enter the house. All the lives in that house were saved. But none dared leave, for if they did they were eligible for the death sentence, be they Egyptian or Israelite. And so they stayed inside until the danger had passed by. But oh, glory to God, when they went out, they were free men!

The Pharaoh of Egypt raised himself from the death bed of his son to issue the command: "Rise up and get you forth from among my people" (Exodus 12:31).

The Ransomed by the Blood

Again it was the blood that had ransomed the hosts of Israel. This day was the day of a new beginning. God said, "This is your New Year's day. From now on you will keep this day in remembrance of the great deliverance which was yours unto all generations" (Exodus 12:2, 24).

It is important to know from this lesson that God has promised a means of deliverance, a place to hide from the destroyer as he stalks the land. The mark of THE BLOOD: that's why Jesus died. But we ourselves must apply His shed Blood to the door of our hearts. Only then will we escape an even greater day of wrath that is appointed for all the earth. It will not be enough to say—

I've done many great deeds
I've tried to do my best
I have made many sacrifices
I've served God a lifetime
I was a member of a church and sang in the choir
and taught Sunday school classes
The only thing that will save us then is the Blood of the Lamb. We must learn to live under His covering and not go out from it. For our life depends on staying hidden in the center of His perfect holy will for our lives.

STUDY QUESTIONS

1. Read Hebrews, chapter 6, and Exodus, chapter 12.

2. Memorize I John 1:7.

3. How was the Mosaic covenant sealed?

4. Why did the destroyer not kill the firstborn of the children of Israel?

5. What kind of lamb was chosen to be slain?

6. What is New Year's Day in the Hebrew calendar?

7. What is the only ransom for sinners?

CHAPTER 5

Life in the Blood

In Leviticus 17:11 we read, "For the life of the flesh is in the blood. And I have given it to you upon the altar to make an atonement for your souls: for it is the blood that maketh an atonement for the soul."

God is saying, "For the life of the body is in its blood, and I have given it to you—for the altar—to expiate for your sins."

Then God adds, "Therefore I said unto the children of Israel, No soul of you shall eat blood, neither shall any stranger that sojourneth among you eat blood" (verse 12).

God wants that man should understand that the eternal stream of life flows through the veins of blood in man and beast. Even the blood of the fowl was to be respected. "And whatsoever man there be of the children of Israel, or the strangers that sojourn among you, which hunteth and catcheth any beast or fowl that may be eaten; he shall even pour out the blood thereof, and cover it with dust" (Leviticus 17:13). God was committing the blood of the fowl and beast back to the earth so the earth could "open her mouth" and receive the blood of her creatures that were slain, like she did for Abel.

God said that if anyone ate the flesh of a beast that had not been properly slain, that one would be unclean (Leviticus 17:15). A punishment of death was decreed on the one who would eat the blood (Genesis 9:6; Leviticus 17:14).

The Law Against Drinking Blood

This law was one of the great laws that was carried over into the laws of the church in New Testament times. When

18

the church elders counseled together in Jerusalem for guidelines they could give the many new converts among the Gentiles, they came to the decision to not enforce circumcision upon them (a dramatic concession for an Israelite to make, and which he could only have made by a divine revelation of God). They were commanded to abstain from 1) pollution of idols, 2) fornication, 3) eating things strangled, and from blood (Acts 15:20). This law is still valid today. We have no freedom or right to annul it.

The Law Against Eating Things Strangled

Here in America, a country built on the laws of the Bible, it is difficult to understand why God commanded them to not eat things strangled. But in foreign countries where I have lived, even in Hong Kong, many Sundays were spent by people gathering together for a "dog feast." They wrap a tight wire or rope around the neck of the animal, strangling it in its blood, and then they cook it. I have been told that the meat is very delicious. It could be; I've never tasted it. I was repulsed by the thought. It became a standing joke whenever our dogs were lost, "It may have ended up in a pot." What saddened me was that sometimes Christians did it, too. We had one sister in our church whom God convicted of it and she stood up to make confession and ask forgiveness publicly.

God has given us the river of blood in the veins of man and beast as a source of life to all His creation. It comes from the source of all life: God, the Almighty Creator.

In the Garden of Eden God forbade man to eat of the tree of the knowledge of good and evil (Genesis 2:17). Since the expulsion man is forbidden to eat the blood of His creation.

The Dome of the Rock

When we take our tour groups on the End-Time

19

Handmaidens' pilgrimage to Israel, we always visit the site of the ancient temple. Standing over the original altar of sacrifices is the Mosque of Omar, or the Dome of the Rock. When you come inside the beautiful building and go down some ancient steps, you will see the actual hole where the blood of the sacrifices was poured into from the altar. Every time I stand there under that opening in the rock, I am overwhelmed with the thought of how many multitudes of animals through the thousands of years from Solomon until 70 AD died for the sins of mankind in this place, and how much blood has flowed. And then I remember Calvary, just a few hundred yards to the north where Jesus hung as the final offering for sin, the Lamb of God who died to take away the sins of the world. And in my heart I hear the refrain of that beautiful old hymn of the church:

> There is a fountain filled with blood
> Drawn from Immanuel's veins;
> And sinners plunged beneath that flood
> Lose all their guilty stains.
>
> —William Cowper

Jesus' Blood Speaks Deliverance Eternally

Yes, this is the Blood that speaks a better message than Abel's (Hebrews 12:24). This is the Blood of God's own beloved Son. The life of the Father is in it. This Blood speaks; it gives forth the vibrations, rays, beams of love, forgiveness, mercy, deliverance, and of the power of a transformed life to all who will accept it as the one and only atonement for all their sins. To reject the Blood is to reject our source of salvation. Satan knows this. That is why he has hated the message of the Blood. He has fought it in every new awakening, every new move of God, every new denomination. He has taken the message of the Blood out of the hymn books, out of the mouths of the preachers and teachers and finally out of the hearts of the people. But the fountain of Blood flows on from the riven side of our Saviour, over mountain, hill, valley, and plain; in desert and city. And wherever man on this sin-cursed earth will humble himself to dip his soul into this "Jordan of God," he shall be made whole and his being shall return to that of the innocency of a child.

Oh beloved, let no one EVER rob from your theology (knowledge of God) the efficaciousness of the Blood of Jesus —the precious Blood of the Son of God (Hebrews 9:11-15).

If God could hear the cry of Abel's blood, how much more can He hear the cry of the Blood of the Son of God. If we disregard it—still God does not.

A Future Age of Innocence

There may come a millenium when man will no more need the shed Blood of Jesus as the source of his justification before God. But even then, man will sing the praises of the slain Lamb of yesterday. We may again enter an age of innocence when no more are men conceived in iniquity and born in sin. Perhaps when Satan is bound a thousand years and none of his imps and demons are working to destroy God's children, and Christ reigns King and Lord over this new heaven and new earth, there will be no need of forgiveness or redemption or atonement, for man will be as the angels— living in an eternally unfallen state. But until that glorious morning breaks, we still must cleave to that "old rugged cross stained with Blood so divine."

STUDY QUESTIONS

1. Read Hebrews, chapter 7.

2. Memorize Leviticus 17:11.

3. Why is man's blood precious?

4. What two things did God command His children not to eat?

5. Why is it a sin to drink blood? Why is it a sin to eat things strangled?

6. Why is the hole in the rock at the temple site significant?

7. In what way does the Blood of Jesus speak better things?

8. What do you think the future age will be like?

CHAPTER 6

Salvation Through the Blood Alone

Our peace and reconciliation with God is not achieved by our good works (Ephesians 2:8, 9). Nor can we ever hope to receive forgiveness by some other mortal dying for us. Listen to what God says through Paul: "And, having made peace through the *Blood of His cross,* by Him [Jesus] to reconcile all things unto Himself [God] ; by Him, I say, whether they be things in earth, or things in heaven" (Colossians 1:20).

God identifies the forgiving, cleansing Blood with that which stained the old rugged cross, the Blood of the Lord Jesus. He goes on to say that through this supreme offering of the body of Christ (through death) we will be presented to God, holy, unblameable and unreprovable (irreproachable) in His sight (Colossians 1:21, 22).

Oh hallelujah! What a beautiful gift of love! What a glorious, full and free salvation! What more could man desire than to be admitted into the bosom of the Father as without blame or reproach! Why does man then still seek for salvation through his own efforts? Why does man pass the suffering Christ by, hanging crucified and bleeding for his sins, and think that he can please God more by rejecting God's gift of salvation and by trying to be his own saviour through the good works he can do?

The Love of God

His only Son to us He gave,
To shed His Blood, our souls to save.
This Precious Blood, it poured like rain;
To cleanse us from our guilty stain.

23

As He hung there upon the tree,
And paid our debt to set us free.
What matchless gift from Heaven above!
It took our Heavenly Father's love
To feel the torture of His Son,
For He alone the battle won.
For millions it was all in vain;
Some other way they try to gain.
In place of Him they trust in work,
And live in fear, in case they shirk.
They have no peace within their soul,
They add man's reason to their goal.
But oh, to know 'twas paid in full;
And we become as pure as wool.
And all our sins as white as snow;
Because His Word declares it so.
My peace, I give it unto you,
To give you strength your whole life through.
You have My word, you are My son,
If you receive what I have done.
Joint heir with Me in Heaven above;
Oh Precious Soul, receive My love.

—R. G. Gurr

The Apostle Peter cries out, ". . . for there is *none other name* under heaven given among men, whereby we *MUST* be saved" (Acts 4:12). Not CAN be, but MUST be. The emphasis is very strong there. As long as you reject Christ's shed Blood as your source of salvation, you are eternally damned. Not until you confess yourself a sinner and ask His Blood to cover you are you safe from the destroyer.

Jesus Offers His Blood to the Father

You cannot get forgiveness from sins by your own efforts. Hebrews 9:22 says, "Without the shedding of blood there is *no* remission for your sins." The writer of Hebrews goes on to explain that Christ has once and for all time offered Himself (Hebrews 9:14) and appeared before God in the HOLY PLACE (of which the tabernacle was only a symbol) to put away sin by the sacrifice of Himself (Hebrews 9:26). There He offered up His shed Blood to the Father for the redemption of the world. Paul says, "This MAN, after He had offered one sacrifice for sins for ever, sat down on the right hand of God. For by one offering He hath perfected for ever them that are sanctified" (Hebrews 10:12, 14).

We have no other source of salvation. Hebrews 12:2 tells us, "Looking unto Jesus, the author and the finisher of our faith; who for the joy that was set before Him endured the cross, despising [having no thought or regard for] the shame, and is set down at the right hand of the throne of God."

Pattern of the Tabernacle

We know that the tabernacle was a symbol of the eternal plan of God, a shadow of heavenly things (Hebrews 8:5). If we want to fully understand the will of God and the ultimate purpose of God, we must trace it in the shadow which God gave to us. For this we turn to the pattern God showed Moses on the mount (Hebrews 8:5).

Blood Not Offered With Leaven

Exodus 23:18, "Thou shalt not offer the blood of my sacrifice with leavened bread." The offering to God of leavened bread was reserved for one particular occasion only: the Feast of Pentecost. In Leviticus 23:17 they were commanded to give God, from their homes, two wave loaves made with fine flour and leaven. Leaven is not only a type of sin; strange to say, it is a type of resurrection life (yeast causes the dough to rise). We know that Pentecost was the outpouring of the abundant life, the resurrection power that raised Jesus from the dead. If we have this resurrection life in us, it will still quicken our mortal bodies by the Holy Spirit. But God does not want to confuse salvation with the baptism of the Holy Spirit. They are two separate works of grace. And so He says, "Thou shalt *not* offer the blood of my sacrifice with leaven." It is a dangerous thing to try to push people into the experience of the baptism of the Holy Spirit and exhort them to speak in tongues if we are not sure about their experience of salvation. I have seen "tongues talking" sinners before. I have heard demons speak from people in strange languages. I do not say this to frighten you, but to warn you. Don't be careless with heavenly things and never try to offer God "strange fire." There is a heavenly pattern and we must be careful to do all things according to it. Remember Satan is an imitator, the master of deceit; but he cannot imitate the godly, holy life.

STUDY QUESTIONS

1. Read Hebrews, chapter 8.

2. Memorize Colossians 1:20.

3. Can we please God by our good works? Can we be redeemed by our good works?

4. Give a reason for your answer.

5. In what way is our salvation glorious?

6. What did Jesus do with His blood? Why?

7. Why was it forbidden to offer blood and leaven together?

8. Why should we be careful about whom we pray for to receive the baptism of the Holy Spirit?

26

CHAPTER 7

The Sprinkled Blood

The blood was used in many ways by the priests. Each of these purposes was given by God to Moses. I feel we would benefit to look more closely into the heavenly pattern which we find in a desert tabernacle.

Blood on the Brazen Altar

Leviticus 5:9, "And he shall sprinkle of the blood of the sin offering upon the side of the altar; and the rest of the blood shall be wrung out at the bottom of the altar: it is a sin offering."

Leviticus 5:10, " . . . and the priest shall make atonement for him for his sin which he hath sinned, and it shall be forgiven him."

The blood on the altar of sacrifice (which is the brazen altar) was for the forgiveness of the sinner.

Blood on the Priesthood

Exodus 29:20, 21, "Then shalt thou kill the ram, and take of his blood, and put it upon the tip of the right ear of Aaron, and upon the tip of the right ear of his sons, and upon the thumb of their right hand, and upon the great toe of their right foot, and sprinkle the blood upon the altar round about. And thou shalt take of the blood that is upon the altar, and of the anointing oil, and sprinkle it upon Aaron, and upon his garments, and upon his sons, and upon the garments of his sons with him: and he shall be hallowed, and his garments, and his sons, and his sons' garments with him."

God would not allow any priest who did not recognize

27

the blood and the anointing to minister unto Him. The priest today who does not bear the mark of the Blood is not God's man—no matter how many high-sounding phrases he uses or how talented and gifted an orator he is, or even how loving a pastor. If you go to a church where the Blood is not honored, you better start seeking God's face about whether you are doing His will. And if you support financially a ministry that is silent concerning the greatest truth of the Holy Scripture, you better know you are paying the way for that which is not God's pattern or religion.

Blood on the Altar of Incense

Exodus 30:10, "And Aaron shall make an atonement upon the horns of it [the altar of incense] once in a year with the blood of the sin offering of atonements: once in the year shall he make atonement upon it throughout your generations: it is most holy unto the Lord."

God commanded the altar of incense, which is a type of the prayers and intercession of the saints, to be cleansed always with the blood of atonement. Let us not think that we have entrance to God if we reject the blood of His Son.

Blood Before the Veil

Leviticus 4:5, 6, "And the priest that is anointed shall take of the bullock's blood and bring it to the tabernacle of the congregation: And the priest shall dip his finger in the blood, and sprinkle the blood seven times before the Lord, before the vail of the sanctuary."

This sprinkling of blood was for the purification of the priest. God had said in chapter 4, verse 3, "If the priest that is anointed do sin according to the sin of the people; then let him bring for his sin . . . a sin offering." And this was the offering he brought. He sprinkled the blood before the veil, on the ground where he had to walk in his ministry to the

Lord, as well as on the altar of incense, the place from which he offered his prayers and praise to God. It was necessary for the priest to walk on the cleansed and blood-washed foundation. And even today, there is *no other* foundation, than that which is laid, which is Christ Jesus.

Blood on the Mercy Seat

Leviticus 16:14, "And he shall take of the blood of the bullock, and sprinkle it with his finger upon the mercy seat eastward; and before the mercy seat shall he sprinkle of the blood seven times." This was behind the veil in the Holy of Holies.

This was the highest and holiest of all offerings. He was making atonement for all Israel, and for the Holy Place which God said was defiled by the uncleanness of the people who lived around it (chapter 16, verse 16). This was Yom Kippur. None dared stay inside the Holy Place when the high priest of Israel went before God with the blood of cleansing in his hand. As he parted the veil and stood before the mercy seat, he stood as the saviour of Israel with the only offering God would recognize—BLOOD. The incense which he had first of all cast into the fire on the altar of incense filled the Holy of Holies, and the cloud of the incense covered the mercy seat "that he die not" (Leviticus 16:13). There, in that high and holy place on the east side, he sprinkled the blood. The east side is the side from where the Prince is coming. He will come in through the Eastern Gate (Ezekiel 44:1-3). He also sprinkled it seven times in front of the mercy seat (Leviticus 16:14). We cannot approach God's mercy without the Blood clearing the way for us.

Blood for the Cleansing of the Leper

Leviticus 14:2, "This shall be the law of the leper in the day of his cleansing: He shall be brought unto the priest:"

29

Two birds were taken. One was killed in an earthen vessel over running water. The living bird was dipped in the blood of the slain one. The leper to be cleansed was sprinkled with the blood seven times, pronounced clean, and the living bird was set free to fly into the open fields.

This was a type of Jesus taking our place, offering up His blood for our healing and cleansing. We must be dipped into the Blood to be pronounced clean. And only then are we truly free from every sin and bondage and condemnation to "fly out into the open field." All because SOMEBODY took our place!

Authority with the Blood

Leviticus 7:33, "He among the sons of Aaron, that offereth up the blood of the peace offerings . . . shall have the right shoulder for his part." The shoulder in scripture always speaks of authority. When Saul went to see Samuel the prophet, Samuel reserved for him the portion of the shoulder at the great feast (I Samuel 9:23, 24). This was because Samuel knew Saul was the one God would anoint to be king. He would put the responsibility of Israel upon Saul's shoulders.

In Isaiah 9:6 we read about the Messiah of Israel: "For unto us a child is born, unto us a son is given: and the government shall be upon His shoulder." This is confirmation that the shoulder speaks of sovereignty, power, and authority.

Jesus carried the cross on His shoulder as He walked the bloody Via Dolorosa. The symbol of His kingdom was the cross He carried, and it has been ever since.

Only the man of God who teaches the true Blood message has the authority of God in his ministry and on his life.

STUDY QUESTIONS

1. Read Hebrews 9 and Leviticus, chapter 14.

2. Memorize Ephesians 2:13.

3. Why was the blood sprinkled on the brazen altar?

4. Why was the blood sprinkled on the priests?

5. Why was the blood sprinkled on the altar of incense?

6. Why was the blood sprinkled before the veil?

7. Why was the blood sprinkled on the mercy seat?

8. How was the leper cleansed?

9. Why did the priests have authority to eat a special portion of meat, and what was it?

CHAPTER 8

The Blood of the Old Covenant

In Exodus 24:8 we read, "And Moses took the blood and sprinkled it on the people and said, Behold the blood of the covenant, which the Lord has made with you . . ." The blood of the Passover Lamb which set the captive slaves of Israel free was the beginning of all sacrifices made under the Mosaic Covenant. From then on, multitudes of thousands of lambs and bullocks and fowl, etc., would have to die for the sins of the people.

In the above scripture we read how Moses sprinkled the people en masse with the blood. When he had finished doing this the heavens were opened to Moses, the priests, and the seventy elders of Israel. They saw the God of Israel, and there was under His feet as it were a paved work of sapphire stone and as it were the body of heaven for clearness (the splendor of the clear sun). And they did eat and drink with God (Exodus 24:10, 11).

How can the priesthood of today have anything to give the people if they are not willing to obey the Bible pattern? These servants of God had a message for Israel because they themselves had been in God's presence. The seventy elders could indeed be elders because they did eat and drink with God. The tragedy today is that many elders are self-made, or manmade, and they are unworthy for this high office because they have never eaten with God. They have nothing to give the people. They have only their own carnal know-how and a lot of self-righteousness, spiritual pride and the spirit of controlling and ruling God's flock. My brother, unless God Himself has put the government of His people upon you, you would do well not to seek such an elevated office.

The Blood of the New Covenant

On that night that Jesus was betrayed He sat with His disciples in an upper room for one last meal together. This has been called "the last supper." It was then, on the eve of His death, that He took the cup of wine in His hands and said, " . . . Drink ye all of it, for this is the blood of the *new covenant* which is shed for many for the remission of sins" (Matthew 26:27, 28).

This was a greater covenant that He was making with man, because it was a greater Blood that was being shed. This was to be an everlasting covenant. The writer of Hebrews says, "Now the God of peace, that brought again from the dead our Lord Jesus, that great shepherd of the sheep, through the Blood of the *everlasting* covenant make you perfect in every good work to do His will . . ." (Hebrews 13:20, 21).

This was the sealing of the final everlasting covenant. This time the Blood being shed was not only the Blood of the Lamb of God, but the Blood of the Shepherd of the sheep.

The Blood Type of Jesus

Oh what glorious secret of God is in the Blood of Jesus!

Every child carries the same blood type as its father. Jesus was born of a virgin when she conceived by a sovereign act of God. The Holy Spirit of God came upon Mary and overshadowed her until she brought forth that "holy thing." What type of Blood flowed in His human body if Jesus did not have an earthly father? He *must* have had the Blood of deity.

For centuries classical mythology has believed that ICHOR, an ethereal fluid, flowed in the veins of the gods. It was a mixture of blood and water. Was it any wonder then, that when the Roman soldier pierced Jesus' side and there flowed from the wound a gush of blood and water the centurion cried in great alarm, "Truly this was the Son of God!"

It was more than the earthquake or the darkened sky that convinced him. I believe it was the sign of water in the precious Blood of Jesus—the Blood of God. It is this same Blood which John said cleanses us from all sin (I John 1:7). Is it any wonder that our sins can be cleansed away, when so great a Blood was shed for them?

A Costly Ransom

I Peter 1:18, 19 says, "We were not redeemed with corruptible things, as silver and gold, . . . but with the precious Blood of Christ, a Lamb without blemish and without spot."

Peter talks a man's language. We are brainwashed to think money can buy anything. But there is one thing that silver and gold—sterling or dollars—cannot buy, and that is our redemption. It can only be purchased through the incorruptible Blood of the Lamb, who verily was foreordained to be our final offering and sacrifice before the foundation of the world and who was manifest in these last times for you (I Peter 1:20).

Paul the Apostle confirms this in Ephesians 1:7, "In *whom* we have redemption through His Blood, the forgiveness of sins, according to the riches of His grace."

Today the sons and wives and husbands of millionaires are kidnapped and held for thousands and even millions of dollars ransom money. Remember, we were born the sons and daughters of God; millionaires have nothing on us. But the evil one kidnapped us and we came into great and terrible bondage. Our cry for deliverance and salvation has gone up to God, until seeing us with the eyes of fatherly love, He sent His Son to pay the *only* ransom price that would set us free. Jesus died in my place that I can be redeemed and restored to my original state in God's kingdom.

STUDY QUESTIONS

1. Read Hebrews, chapter 10.

2. Memorize I Peter 1:19.

3. What happened after Moses sprinkled the altar with the blood?

4. In what way can that be applied to today's churches?

5. In what way was the new covenant greater than the old one?

6. What was Jesus besides the "Lamb"?

7. What is ICHOR?

8. In what way have we been kidnapped and ransomed?

CHAPTER 9

The Holy Cup

Because Jesus identified His own Blood with that of the cup of communion, it is important for us to understand more about this special and blessed sacrament.

In I Corinthians 11:27 Paul says, "Whosoever eateth this bread and drinketh this cup of the Lord, unworthily, is guilty of the Body and Blood of the Lord."

These are startling and frightening words. None of us want to be guilty of taking the cup of Jesus' holy communion in an unworthy manner, nor do we want to be guilty of His suffering Body and shed Blood.

Paul says that he that eateth and drinketh unworthily, eateth and drinketh damnation (or condemnation or judgment) to himself (I Corinthians 11:29). It seems there is *no* excuse for ignorance.

When we come to the table of God to eat and drink with God we are doing what the seventy elders did in the holy mount with Moses and the priests of God. "Then went up Moses, and Aaron, Nadab, and Abihu, and seventy of the elders of Israel: And they saw the God of Israel: and there was under his feet as it were a paved work of a sapphire stone, and as it were the body of heaven in his clearness. And upon the nobles of the children of Israel he laid not his hand: also they saw God, and did eat and drink" (Exodus 24:9-11).

God wants that we should come with clean hands and a pure heart. He says, "But let a man examine himself [check and test himself]" (I Corinthians 11:28). This is the hardest thing to do! But God expects us to take spiritual inventory before we take the holy communion.

There must be a reason why so many of God's children are sick when His atonement has provided healing for us.

And it seems like Paul has found one of the reasons: "For THIS CAUSE many are weak and sickly among you, and many sleep" (I Corinthians 11:30). This "sleep" means more than slumber; it refers to the sleep we call death. Paul received this revelation from the Lord, and that's why he could speak with such confidence. No doubt he had asked God the same question so many of us have asked Him: Why are so many Christians sick, when the Word says, "... and with His stripes we *are* healed?" (Isaiah 53:5; I Peter 2:24). And God gave him the reason: they approached the table of God with unconfessed sins, unrepentant hearts, and with unforgiveness to their fellow man. In so doing, they were bringing damnation (or condemnation, or judgment) upon their bodies. The bread, which was the Body of Christ broken for our healing, worked the opposite way; it brought sickness. And the cup, which was the Blood of the Lord, brought not the sense of forgiveness but even greater condemnation and judgment.

The "Closed Communion"

In some denominations there is what is called "closed communion." This is where only the members of that particular group can take the communion together. Anyone coming from another similar (closed communion) group must have a letter of recommendation by their elders. While I do not advocate such a policy (for who are we to judge who is worthy?), I can understand how this might have come about because of the truth of Paul's revelation. Men of God have felt a responsibility in serving communion to those whose lives they were not sure of, so they wanted to keep from causing condemnation to themselves and damnation to others.

The Power of Confession

Yes, the Word of God gives us the perfect way—LOVE.

This is the more excellent way (I Corinthians 12:31-13:13). With true love in our hearts we CAN come into the presence of God. Love will enable us to forgive, to repent, and to confess.

Leviticus 5:5, "And it shall be, when he is guilty in one of these things, that he shall confess that he hath sinned in THAT thing." Only you yourself know what THAT thing is; but THAT is the thing you must make confession of.

James 5:16 says, "Confess your sins one to another, and pray one for another, THAT YE MAY BE HEALED." Here is the very thing Paul is trying to tell us: confession of sins brings healing.

Matthew 7:4, "Or how wilt thou say to thy brother, Let me pull out the mote (dust) out of thine eye, and, behold, a beam [a chip] is in thine own eye?"

So many are critical because they are blinded by the chips in their own eyes. God needs to give us clarity of vision so that we can find our neighbor in the Spirit. When we do, we will also be given the grace to examine ourselves and find ourselves in the Spirit. The hardest person to know is oneself. It's too humbling, and yet it is the one and only door to greatness.

Jesus said, "If thy brother shall trespass against thee, go and tell him his fault between thee and him alone: if he shall hear thee, thou hast gained thy brother" (Matthew 18:15).

Self Examination

I have seen missionaries die of terrible diseases because they could not make things right with their brother or sister in Christ.

I remember when God first gave me this message to preach on the mission field, I knew for whom God had given me this "strong meat." It was holy communion Sunday. With tears I pled from the pulpit, "Make things right before you take the holy communion!" God's anointing was upon me in a special way. I knew how for years this dear one had carried a root of bitterness against another missionary who was hard to get along with. But I felt God was not going to permit it any longer. When I finished and sat down, the communion service began. I watched to see if she would accept the Spirit's message. She was the leading missionary, and if she did not take communion everyone would see it. I prayed for her to have grace to make things right before she partook. When I saw her reach out for the bread, my heart broke. All my tears and prayers could not avail. It was her LAST holy communion; she died soon after. And yet that morning she was the picture of health. Because she was my friend and I had listened to her stories and had "gossiped" along, great conviction fell on me. I felt that although I had not hated these troublemakers, still I was an "accessory after the fact" because I had listened. I felt as if God would take me next. A great fear from God fell on me. I asked God to help me to examine myself. For one week God revealed to me all whom I had to ask forgiveness of. There were so many that if He had shown them to me all at once, I couldn't have done it. Some were harder than others. I carried one letter in my purse for three days until I had the courage to post it. When the last confession had been made, the sweet peace of God filled my heart and I felt so clean!

The only one you harm by your hurt, anger, hate, and unforgiveness is yourself. Don't allow bitter grievances from bygone days to bring damnation on yourself. Do yourself a good turn—FORGIVE!

Healing in the Communion

On the other hand, we have witnessed and personally experienced the most marvelous miracles of healing take place through the Holy Communion. It is an act of obedience. Jesus said, "This do in remembrance of Me" (Luke 22:19). By observing this Christian rite we are calling to

39

remembrance Jesus' death. In that death is the mighty key for our complete atonement. Jesus died for our *full* salvation, body, soul, and spirit.

Psalm 103:2, 3 says, "Bless the Lord, O my soul, and forget not all His benefits: Who *forgiveth* all thine iniquities; who *healeth* all thy diseases." All my sins and infirmities were laid on Jesus Christ when He suffered those dark hours of His passion.

As we partake of the broken bread, which symbolizes His body which was broken for us, we are doing it as an act of faith, believing He *suffered* that we do not need to suffer. By His stripes we were healed.

He *wore the crown of thorns* that pierced His brain so that my mind can be free of all mental torment or anxiety.

He *died* that I might live.

I Peter 2:24, "Who his own self bare our sins in His own body on the tree, that we, being dead to sins, should live unto righteousness: by whose stripes ye were healed."

This is the full extent of what His atonement meant for everyone. As we take the bread and the wine we are bearing witness that we are taking Him as our Great Healer and sin-bearer.

Next time you take Holy Communion, believe that this is true, and if your heart is clean of sin and you have made restitution with your brother, expect a miracle of healing to take place in your body.

STUDY QUESTIONS

1. Read Hebrews, chapter 11, and I Corinthians 11:23-33.

2. Memorize James 5:16.

3. In what way can holy communion bring either blessing or damnation?

4. What happens when we are damned because of disobedience?

5. What is a "closed communion?"

6. Why is confession good for us?

7. Why is it hard for us to examine ourselves?

8. What are the wages of sin?

9. Explain how the holy communion rite can give you a miracle of healing.

CHAPTER 10

The Curse in the Blood-Line

Paul said in 2 Corinthians 6:14, "Be ye not unequally yoked together with unbelievers: for what fellowship hath righteousness with unrighteousness? And what communion hath light with darkness?" And let me say right here, you can love and forgive and have compassion on children of darkness *without* having communion and fellowship with them. It's better for your soul to stay away from some people.

Paul gave this warning because he knew the believer was the temple where God dwelt, whereas in the heart of the sinner there are many idols. The prophet Amos said in 3:3, "Can two walk together except they be agreed?" Marriage is a 'walking-together.' It's so important to marry the one whom God has created to be your life's partner. In this day many foolish, reckless people throw their lives' callings away by being joined together in holy matrimony with an unholy vessel.

The Pedigree Race

We must never forget that the one we marry will be the father or mother of our unborn child. When God wanted to call out a certain people, He arranged for a pedigree family to be parents to it. Jacob's parents were first cousins (Isaac and Rebecca). His grandparents were half-brother and sister (Abraham and Sarah). Why did God do this? Because He wanted a pure people with pure blood. Abraham's father Terah, who lived in the Ur of the Chaldees, was the first to break away from idol-worshipping religions that the people had fallen snare to. And God wanted that the descendants of this godly man would be the fathers and mothers of the future chosen generation. God picked Isaac's wife and God picked Jacob's. From this royal line came many kings and prophets, and finally our Saviour—the Lion of the tribe of Judah.

God is not a respecter of persons when it comes to salvation. It's for all who will call upon Him. But God is a respecter of persons when it comes to choosing who is His elect:

Isaac was His elect; Ishmael wasn't. Both had the same father.

Jacob was His elect; Esau wasn't. Both had the same mother and father.

Why was this? Because Ishmael was contaminated by the Egyptian bondwoman Hagar and Esau was contaminated by his wives, the daughters of Heth, a nomadic idolatrous prince. God knew He could not use their children because the blood line was impure.

The Curse Unto the Third and Fourth Generation

Exodus 34:7, "Keeping mercy for thousands, forgiving iniquity and transgression and sin, and that will by no means clear the guilty; visiting the iniquity of the fathers upon the children, and upon the children's children, unto the third and to the fourth generation."

Leviticus 26:39, "In the iniquities of their fathers shall they pine away."

Numbers 14:23, "And your children shall wander in the wilderness forty years and bear your whoredoms." The children had to suffer for the unbelief of their parents.

Produce After Their Kind

When God created the animals and fowl, He commanded them to produce AFTER THEIR KIND. This law still holds true today. Both man and beast produce after their own kind. That's why it's important who you marry, for that one will graft into your descendants all that he and his ancestors ever were. Only a sovereign act of God, where in answer to prayer, can God break the laws of nature and the command He spoke by His own mouth. Only then can He reach out and touch the life of the one whose blood line has a special curse on it.

Cain fathered the ones that God had to destroy in the flood. Don't think that *you* can change that man or woman. You are never going to do it. Don't mingle your pure blood with that of a sinful cursed generation. It's better never to marry and have children than to produce after the kind of Cain.

A professor of one of the most well-known European Bible schools said people have discovered that after major blood transfusions the character of the recipients was completely altered and permanently affected. These cases have been studied and the fact has been scientifically proven. What else could this be than the curse in the blood stream handed down or transferred by blood transfusion.

The Greatest Sin

Many times we wonder which of the deadly sins is the greatest. It is impossible for us to judge. God alone knows the motives of the heart and the weaknesses of each person which are inherited and which we try so hard to overcome.

As I search through the Word of God, there seems to be one sin that grieves God more than any other, and that is the taking of another life. The voice of God thunders from Mount Sinai, "Thou shalt not kill!" In Numbers 35:30, 31, He said, "Whoso killeth any person, the murderer shall be put to death by the mouth of witnesses: . . . Moreover ye shall take no satisfaction for the life of a murderer, which is guilty of death: but he shall be surely put to death." Murder carried the sentence of death in God's book of rules.

Murder Pollutes the Land

God said that the killing of another polluted the land. Numbers 35:33, 34, "So ye shall not pollute the land wherein ye are: for the blood defileth the land: and the land cannot be cleansed of the blood that is shed therein, but by the blood of him that shed it. Defile not therefore the land which ye shall inhabit, wherein I dwell: for I the Lord dwell among the children of Israel."

When God gave our fathers the land of America, they brought their Bibles along and built by the rules of the Good Book. The sentence for murder was capital punishment. This has been abolished in many states. Thinking we are progressing in thought and improving our country's laws, we are suffering the murderer to live. Yes, even the mass murderer. By this act we defile the land God has given us.

Euthanasia Lies Ahead

Our forefathers honored and respected their parents and in so doing lived long upon the land which the Lord their God gave them. Today our America is full of old mamas and papas who are forgotten by their children and their children's children. Some are existing in rundown "Old Folks' Homes" with barely enough to eat and no love, doped with drugs to keep them in a state of stupor so they will not be troublesome. Others exist on the streets of our big cities, living in doorways and hovels. Tomorrow it will be worse: euthanasia is being considered and even desired to rid the land of those who are only a liability and an expense. If the social pension breaks down, which it is on the verge of, the elderly who pay their way through these resources will be thrown out and euthanasia will become the IN thing as volunteers will be encouraged to die for the young and the vital citizens. And many will "volunteer" to die, thinking they are doing God and mankind a good deed. For this, judgment will come because of the genocidal blood offering.

The Blood of the Innocents

The land is already polluted by the blood of our innocents. God says in Jeremiah 2:34, "In thy skirts are found the blood of the souls of the poor innocents." There is more killing taking place in our American hospital sterile delivery rooms than the bloodiest battlefield of all time. Last year 1.1 million of our unborn infants were murdered in their mothers' wombs. And God says, "Yet they say, 'I have not sinned' " (Jeremiah 2:35).

The life of the human is in the blood. Instruments of torture are pushed into the wombs of the mothers, tearing their babies apart, spilling their blood out of them.

Every life is a gift of God, and if you take a life and hinder it from fulfilling its sojourn, you are a murderer. It makes no difference what the age of the soul is which you cut off from life, murder is murder. And God said the only way that the land can be cleansed of bloodshed is by the blood of him that shed it. Sometimes it seems to me that God will cause the curse of euthanasia to come on those tomorrow who abort their children today.*

The tract, "Thou Shalt Not Kill," is available from us for $.05.

46

STUDY QUESTIONS

1. Read Hebrews, chapter 12.

2. Memorize Romans 5:9 and 2 Corinthians 6:14.

3. Why should we be careful of whom we marry?

4. What is carried in the blood line from one generation to another?

5. Tell about a certain pedigree race. How did it begin and why?

6. What does the command, "produce after your kind" mean?

7. What sin grieves God the most? And why?

8. Name three ways America is in danger of bringing down the wrath of God upon herself.

CHAPTER 11

Love Is in the Blood

I want to ask you a question. In I John 1:7 it says, "The Blood of Jesus Christ, His Son, cleanseth us from all sin." Why does the Blood of Jesus Christ have power to take away our sins? Why not some other part of Jesus' body? Why not His mind, His liver, His gall within Him? Why does it have to be His Blood?

That's because life is in the blood (Leviticus 17:11). Blood is a living substance. If you would ask a scientist what blood is, he might give you many answers. Scientists lately have been making an extensive study about blood because they saw there is something peculiar and supernatural about blood. They have come to the conclusion that blood is congealed light. In other words, in the body of man there are veins, and in these veins a red substance is flowing that is none other than light—light that has become mystically congealed. How did it happen? What was man's original state when he was created? When God created Adam, what gave him the potential of an eternal life?

Why Adam and Eve Were Perfect

I believe that in the veins of our brother Adam and our sister Eve was not blood like mine but rather, because of their perfection, there was the very light of God flowing, coursing up and down from head to foot in their whole being. And this light gave them eternal life. This was the glory that they lost when they fell from their former state. And the curse that fell on them and their descendants was that this river of light turned into congealed light and today blood still has light in it, but it is under the curse of death.

48

There is life in every man's blood; but in the Blood of Jesus there is abundant life, life right from the throne of God. It was the Blood of the Father that flowed in Jesus' veins which He offered up for our transgressions. What is the difference between the love of God and that of a mortal man? God is Love! It was a fountain of love that flowed through the veins of Jesus. That is what made the Blood of Jesus a pure, sinless offering. It was the essence of love flowing out to cover our sins. Love, liquified, flowed in the veins of Jesus. And as that fountain of Blood flowed from His wounds, it was a fountain of love, a stream of everlasting life.

That is why the Blood of Jesus is almighty. That is why it has never-dying power. That is why, two thousand years after it was shed, it still has the power to take men's sins away. It still has the power to change a cruel, hard, evil man into a man of kindness. Because when the Blood of God through Jesus covers a man, he is enfolded in love and that love transforms him and drives out the evil, even the evil of many generations.

And this is the ONLY thing that can transform a person and deliver him from the sins and weaknesses and curses of his forefathers. Yes, beloved, the life is in the blood because the love of God is in it.

"We know that we have passed from death unto life, because we love the brethren. He that loveth not his brother abideth in death" (I John 3:14). The Lord wants you to pour that river of healing, cleansing, purifying love through your body. When that happens, you will be fulfilling that which you must fulfill if you want everlasting life; for life is in the Blood.

How Do We Drink Jesus' Blood?

Jesus said, "Except ye eat the flesh of the Son of man, and drink His Blood, ye have no life in you" (John 6:53). What did He mean? He didn't mean that we are to drink

49

blood. We are forbidden to do this. This is what He meant: we must drink and partake of His life-giving stream of *Love*. Unless we have his Love, we do not have His life. Jesus said, "He that drinketh my Blood dwelleth in me, and I in him" (John 6:56). Or, in other words, if thou hast love, thou shalt dwell in Him and He in thee. When we drink of THAT "Blood" (the life-giving stream of Love), we are actually just taking the love of God and making it a part of our life.

Many are waiting for the transformation, the rapture, the translation, the raising up, or the manifestation of the sons of God—or even the Kingdom on earth. Call it what you may, the terminology may differ but the ultimate result will be the same. This is the hope of the children of God. And yet we can't have this without the Blood of Jesus. The Blood of Jesus is the manifestation of God's Love and God's Son.

I believe that the Blood of Jesus is going to become more powerful in the end-time, more powerful than in the day it poured from His veins, until it will touch our very bodies. And not only will our spirits be changed, but our bodies will be changed. Not only will your spirit have eternal life, but your body will be quickened to live forever. That is the power of the message of the Blood. Drink His Blood, absorb His love into your innermost being. It will immortalize your body, and whether you live or die, He has promised, "I will raise you up at the last day" (John 6:54).

STUDY QUESTIONS

1. Read Hebrews, chapter 13.

2. Memorize Hebrews 13:12.

3. Why does Jesus' Blood cleanse us from sin and not another part of His anatomy?

4. Why were Adam and Eve perfect?

5. What is different about the Blood of Jesus from other men?

6. Why does love bring life and hate bring death? Quote a scripture that confirms this.

7. What is the power that will translate us?

8. In what way do we drink Jesus' Blood?

CHAPTER 12

Review

Let us have a brief review:

Hebrews 12:24
> The Blood of Jesus speaketh better things. This is the gospel message, the glad tidings the world needs.

Hebrews 13:20, 21
> The Blood of Jesus makes us perfect in every good work to do His will.

I John 1:7
> The Blood of Jesus cleanseth us from all sin.

Ephesians 2:13
> We are made nigh to God by the Blood of Jesus.

I Peter 1:18, 19
> We are redeemed with the precious Blood of Jesus.

Romans 5:9
> We are justified by the Blood of Jesus.

Hebrews 13:12
> We are sanctified by the Blood of Jesus.

Ephesians 1:7
> We have redemption through the Blood of Jesus.

Colossians 1:20
> We are reconciled through the Blood of Jesus.

Revelation 1:5
> We are washed from our sins by the Blood of Jesus.

Is it any wonder that Satan hates the blood? When we see that the Blood of Jesus completely destroys his kingdom, we can understand why he fights it.

Blood, the Theme of the Redeemed

Let us lift the wings of our feeble imagination and leave our earth-bound thinking long enough to ascend up, up, up into the presence of the Eternal One and the company of saints so great no man can number. The angels are standing hushed, their wings folded as we arrive. They are listening to a song, a song so beautiful that it seems we would die with emotion because of its grandeur. The voices of multitudes of redeemed from every kindred, tongue, people, and nation are lifted up in unison, overflowing in praises to God.

Hear the theme of the singing of these immortals: "Thou art worthy . . . , for Thou wast slain, and hast redeemed us to God by Thy Blood, out of every kindred, and tongue, and people, and nation" (Revelation 5:9). Their sweet music fills the farthest corridors of heaven; it echoes through the palaces of the patriarchs and floats across the sea of glass, out into the outer edge of Paradise. Oh, what beauty! Oh, what glory! And I shall join in that song and sing it also, for I, too, have been redeemed by the precious Blood of the Lamb.

Satan is Defeated

Suddenly a great silence falls over the vast multitude—a holy hush. The harps are stilled, the trumpets are silent. Every face looks with expectation toward the throne. The report is being given the saints of the latest news from planet earth. The great dragon, the master deceiver which deceiveth the whole world, has tried to ascend to the heavens. But Michael and his angels have gone out and fought with him and overcome him. Satan has been defeated. A roar of praise fills the air, and then again is silenced as a loud voice begins to speak:

"Now is come salvation and strength and the kingdom of our God, and the power of His Christ [the authority of His

Messiah!], for the accuser of our brethren is cast down, which accused him before our God day and night. And they overcame him [Satan] BY THE BLOOD OF THE LAMB AND BY THE WORD OF THEIR TESTIMONY; AND THEY LOVED NOT THEIR LIVES UNTO DEATH" (Revelation 12:10, 11).

Yes, they loved not their lives better than death. Their love was the pure and holy love that is ready to give itself as a sacrifice. Ready to be a poured-out offering even as their Lord and Saviour was a poured-out offering for them.

The Blood-washed Martyrs Come Home

Suddenly, as if by instinct, the great company parts and far in the distance we see angels bringing up another great host of people arrayed in spotless, radiant white. The sight of them as they approach almost dazzles our eyes.

Someone asks, "What are these that are arrayed in white robes? And from where are they coming?" We stand silently, the victors' palms in our hands. The twenty-four elders have fallen before the throne on their faces. We gaze with admiration at this beautiful host in white: men, women, children, and babies make up the number. There is a glow of great joy on their faces. Many have their hands raised in worship to the Lord. Some still have the tear stains on their faces, others bear the marks of their suffering. And then the answer comes. Listen!

"These are they which came out of great tribulation, and have washed their robes, and made them white in the Blood of the Lamb!" (Revelation 7:9-14).

Yes, beloved, even martyrdom does not make us worthy to come into the throne room of God. To give our lives, to suffer, be tortured, be imprisoned, and to serve God for a lifetime is all good—but not enough. We must be wearing robes that have been washed in the precious Blood of the Lamb. When we make our entrance into eternity, only the ones whose hearts are sprinkled with the Blood of Jesus, only the ones whose robes have been washed in His Blood, will be given the royal welcome by the One who sitteth on the throne judging all nations, and who gave His Son to die and shed His Blood for the redemption of these nations.

> *Let the Blood of the Lamb cover me,
> Let the truth of His word set me free.
> Let the power of His Blood
> Fill me with His light and love
> That the world will see Jesus in me.
>
> —words by Anita Matula

---

* Sung to the tune, "Let The Love of My God Shine Through Me."

End-Time Handmaidens recommends with this Bible Study the cassette tape G-HF-85, ONLY JESUS' BLOOD CAN STAY THE PLAGUE, by Gwen Shaw. $4.45 (postage included).

(Please turn page.)

STUDY QUESTIONS

1. Read Revelation, chapters 5, 7, 12.

2. Memorize Ephesians 1:7 and Revelation 12:11.

3. Quote from memory all the verses you were asked to memorize: Hebrews 12:24, Romans 6:12, Hebrews 13:20-21, I John 1:7, Leviticus 17:11, Colossians 1:20, Ephesians 2:13, I Peter 1:19, James 5:16, Romans 5:9, 2 Corinthians 6:14, Hebrews 13:12, Ephesians 1:7, and Revelation 12:11.

4. Why does Satan hate the Blood of Jesus?

5. In what way does he fight it?

6. What is the song of heaven that the angels can't sing?

7. How did the saints defeat Satan?

8. Does martyrdom make us worthy of heaven? What gives us entrance?

9. What is the eternal theme song of the redeemed?

The Dome of the Rock

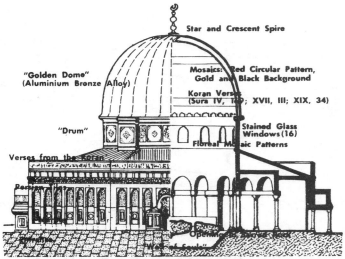

Star and Crescent Spire

"Golden Dome"
(Aluminium Bronze Alloy)

Mosaics: Red Circular Pattern,
Gold and Black Background

Koran Verses
(Sura IV, 169; XVII, III; XIX, 34)

"Drum"

Stained Glass
Windows (16)

Floreal Mosaic Patterns

Verses from the Koran

Persian Tiles

Opening into "Cave of Souls"

Rock of Moriah: Tradition — History: Abraham prepares Isaac for sacrifice on Moriah: David erects altar to God: Site for Temple's Holy of Holies: Destruction — Babylon, Rome: Mohammed ascends to heaven from Rock: 691, Abd el-Malik completes Dome of the Rock: Crusaders — Templum Domini: 1967 — Jews recapture Temple Mount.

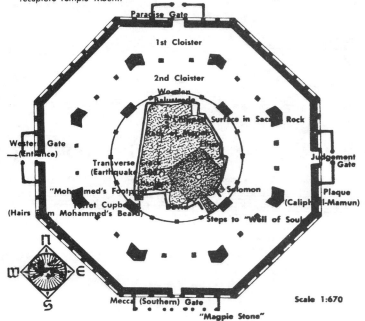

Paradise Gate

1st Cloister

2nd Cloister

Wooden
Balustrade

Climbing Surface in Sacred Rock

Rock of Moriah

Western Gate
(Entrance)

Judgement
Gate

Transverse Crack
(Earthquake?)

"Mohammed's Footprint"

Turret Cupboard
(Hairs from Mohammed's Beard)

Seal of Solomon

Plaque
(Caliph al-Mamun)

Steps to "Well of Souls"

Mecca (Southern) Gate

"Magpie Stone"

Scale 1:670

Lord, I Receive

Words and Music by
Madeline Feldman
Arr. by Dorothy Buss

The Love of My God

G. R. S.

GWEN R. SHAW

Let the love of my God shine thru me.
Strah - le Deine Lie - be aus durch mein Herz.
Let the Blood of the Lamb co—ver me.

Let the beau - ty of Je - sus men see.
Lass der Welt Je - su Schoen - heit nur sehen.
Let the truth of His word set me free.

Let the pat - tern of the Son be the One, the on - ly
Lass das Vor - bild Got - tes Sohn Durch mein gan - zes Le - ben
Let the pow - er of His Blood fill me with His light and

one that men will see in me.
gehen Strah - le aus Dei - ne Lie - be durch mich.
love that the world will see Je - sus in me.

Ad 1

CLASSIC ANOINTED BIBLE STUDIES

BEHOLD THE BRIDEGROOM COMETH!—*Gwen Shaw*. A Bible study on the soon return of Jesus Christ. With so many false teachings these days, it is important that we realize how imminent the rapture of the saints of God really is ....#100-37 $6.50

ENDUED WITH LIGHT TO REIGN FOREVER — *Gwen Shaw*. This deeply profound Bible study reveals the characteristics of the eternal, supernatural, creative light of God as found in His Word. The "Father of Lights," created man in His image. He longs for man to step out of darkness and into His light ....#101-71 $6.00

GOD'S END-TIME BATTLE-PLAN—*Gwen Shaw*. This study on spiritual warfare gives you the biblical weapons for spiritual warfare such as victory through dancing, shouting, praising, uplifted hands, marching, etc. It has been a great help to many who have been bound by tradition ....#102-35 $8.00

IT'S TIME FOR REVIVAL—*Gwen Shaw*. A Bible Study on Revival that not only gives scriptural promises of the end-time Revival, but also presents the stories of revivals in the past and the revivalists whom God used. It will stir your heart and encourage you to believe for great revival ......#103-24 $7.75

OUR MINISTERING ANGELS—*Gwen Shaw*. A scriptural Bible study on the topic of angels. Angels will be playing a more and more prominent part in these last days. We need to understand about them and their ministry ....#104-87 $7.50

POUR OUT YOUR HEART—*Gwen Shaw*. A wonderful Bible study on travailing prayer. The hour has come to intercede before the throne of God. The call to intercession is for everyone, and we must carry the Lord's burden and weep for the lost so that the harvest can be brought in quickly ....#105-16 $3.75

REDEEMING THE LAND—*Gwen Shaw*. This important teaching will help you know your authority through the Blood of Jesus to dislodge evil spirits, break the curse, and restore God's blessing upon the land. A Bible study on spiritual warfare..#108-61 $9.50

THE FINE LINE—*Gwen Shaw*. This Bible study clearly magnifies the "fine line" difference between the soul realm and the spirit realm. Both are intangible and therefore cannot be discerned with the five senses, but must be discerned by the Holy Spirit and the Word of God. A must for the deeper Christian..#101-91 $6.00

THE POWER OF THE PRECIOUS BLOOD—*Gwen Shaw*. A Bible study on the Blood of Jesus. The author shares how it was revealed to her how much Satan fears Jesus' Blood. This Bible study will help you overcome and destroy the works of Satan in your life and the lives of loved ones ....#105-18 $4.00

THE POWER OF PRAISE—*Gwen Shaw*. When God created the heavens and earth He was surrounded by praise. Miracles happen when holy people praise a Holy God! Praise is the language of creation. If prayer can move the hand of God, how much more praise can move Him! ....#400-66 $5.00

Ad 2

YE SHALL RECEIVE POWER FROM ON HIGH *Gwen Shaw*. This is a much needed foundational teaching on the Baptism of the Holy Spirit. It will enable you to teach this subject, as well as to understand these truths more fully yourself...#107-37 $5.00

YOUR APPOINTMENT WITH GOD—*Gwen Shaw*. A Bible study on fasting. Fasting is one of the most neglected sources of power over bondages of Satan that God has given the Church. The author's experiences are shared in this Bible study in a way that will change your life ....#107-40 $4.50

IN-DEPTH BIBLE STUDIES

FORGIVE AND RECEIVE—An In-Depth Bible Study on Philemon for the Serious Student of God's Word—*Gwen Shaw*. This Bible Study is a lesson to the church on the much-needed truths of forgiveness and restoration. The epistle to Philemon came from the heart of Paul who had experienced great forgiveness ....#102-01 $7.00

GRACE ALONE—An In-Depth Bible Study on Galatians for the Serious Student of God's Word—*Gwen Shaw*. This study teaches the reader to gain freedom in the finished work of the Cross by forsaking works which cannot add to salvation and live by *Grace Alone* ....#108-47 $13.00

MYSTERY REVEALED—An In-Depth Bible Study on Ephesians for the Serious Student of God's Word—*Gwen Shaw*. Search the depths of God's riches in one of Paul's most profound epistles, "to the praise of His glory!" Learn the "mystery" of the united Body of Christ.......#104-53 $15.00

OUR GLORIOUS HEAD—An In-Depth Bible Study on Colossians for the Serious Student of God's Word—*Gwen Shaw*. This book teaches vital truths for today, assisting the reader in discerning false teachings, when the philosophies of men are being promoted as being the truths of God. Jesus Christ is the Head of His Body ....#104-85 $9.00

THE CATCHING AWAY!—An In-Depth Bible Study on First and Second Thessalonians —*Gwen Shaw*. This is a very timely Bible Study because Jesus is coming soon! The book of I Thessalonians explains God's revelation to Paul on the rapture of the saints. II Thessalonians reveals what will happen after the rapture when the antichrist takes over ....#100-88 $13.00

THE LOVE LETTER—An In-Depth Bible Study on Philippians for the Serious Student of God's Word—*Gwen Shaw*. Another of Gwen Shaw's expository Bibles Studies on the books of the Bible. This study of the letter to the first church of Europe will give the reader an understanding of Paul's great love for the church that was born out of his suffering ....#103-99 $9.00

BIBLE COURSE

THE TRIBES OF ISRAEL—*Gwen Shaw*. This popular and well-loved study on the thirteen tribes of Israel will show you your place in the spiritual tribes in these last days. Better understand yourself and others through the study of this Bible Course ....#106-70 $45.00

HASTENING OUR REDEMPTION — *Gwen Shaw*. All of Heaven and Earth are waiting for the Body of Christ to rise up in maturity and reclaim what we lost in the Fall of Man. Applying the Blood of Jesus is the key to *Hastening Our Redemption* ....#116-53 $1.50

IT CAN BE AVERTED — *Gwen Shaw*. Many people today are burdened and fearful over prophecies of doom and destruction. However, the Bible is clear that God prefers mercy over judgment when His people humble themselves and pray ....#116-85 $1.50

KAIROS TIME — *Gwen Shaw*. That once in a lifetime opportunity—that second, or minute, or hour, or year, or even longer, when a golden opportunity is sovereignly given to us by the Almighty. What we do with it can change our lives and possibly even change the world ....#200-06 $1.50

KNOWING ONE ANOTHER IN THE SPIRIT—*Gwen Shaw*. Experience great peace as you learn to understand the difficulties your friends, enemies and loved ones face that help to form their character. *"Wherefore henceforth know we no man after the flesh.."* (II Corinthians 5:16a). An anointed message in booklet form ....#103-62 $1.50

THE CRUCIFIED LIFE—*Gwen Shaw*. When you suffer and you know the cause is not your own sin, for you have searched your heart before God; then you must accept that it is God doing a new thing in your life. Let joy rise up within you because you are a partaker of Christ's suffering ....#115-61 $1.50

THE MASTER IS COME AND CALLETH FOR THEE — *Gwen Shaw*. Read about how the Lord called Gwen Shaw to begin the ministry of the End-Time Handmaidens and Servants. Perhaps the Master is also calling you into His service. Bring Him the fragments of your life — He will put them together again. An anointed message booklet ....#104-31 $1.50

WOMEN OF THE BIBLE SERIES

EVE—MOTHER OF US ALL — *Gwen Shaw*. Discover the secrets of one of the most neglected and misunderstood stories in history ....#117-50 $4.50

MIRIAM—THE PROPHETESS — *Gwen Shaw*. The first female to lead worship, the first woman given the title "Leader" of God's people by the Lord ....#M400-67 $7.50

SARAH—PRINCESS OF ALL MANKIND — *Gwen Shaw*. Feel the heartbeat and struggles of this woman who left so great an impact for all time ....#117-51 $4.50

REBEKAH—THE BRIDE — *Gwen Shaw*. The destiny of the world was determined when she says three simple words, "I will go!" ......#117-52 $4.50

LEAH AND RACHEL—THE TWIN WIVES OF JACOB — *Gwen Shaw*. You will feel their dreams, their pains, their jealousies ....#200-46 $4.50

BOOKS PUBLISHED BY ENGELTAL PRESS

ATTITUDES IN THE BEATITUDES — *Esther Rollins.* Esther taught this anointed course on the Beatitudes as a guest teacher at our School of Ministry and an instructor of the Word of God for 50 years. Both basic and profound, this dynamic teaching is full of insight for the Christian walk ....#115-72 $5.95

BANISHED FOR FAITH — *Emil Waltner.* The stirring story of the courageous forefathers of Gwen Shaw, the Hutterite Mennonites, who were banished from their homeland and suffered great persecution for their faith. Republished with an index and epilogue by Gwen Shaw ....#100-33 $12.95

BECOMING A SERVANT — *Robert Baldwin.* Learn what is on God's heart about servanthood. We must learn to serve before we can be trusted to lead. If you want to be great in God's Kingdom, learn to be the servant of all ....#118-55 $2.00

FOOTPRINTS — *Larry Hunt.* A collection of poems and stories reflecting the hand of God upon this humble pastor during 35 years of ministry ....#114-25 $3.75

FROM DUST TO GLORY — *June Lewis.* The Lord intends more than just salvation for us. He is making vessels of eternal Glory if we submit to Him. A collection of poems and stories reflecting the hand of God upon this humble pastor during 35 years of ministry ....#102-07 $7.50

HOLY ANN — *Helen Bingham.* This humble Irish woman moved the arm of God through simple faith and prevailing prayer. Read these modern miracles that are told like a story from the Old Testament. The record of a lifetime of answered prayer ....#110-38 $4.95

IT WAS WORTH IT ALL — *Elly Matz.* The story of a beautiful woman whose courage will inspire you. Feel HER heart as she tells of her starving father, the young Communist engineer she married, the villages mysteriously evacuated, the invading German army, the concentration camp where she was a prisoner, and her escape into freedom ....#115-70 $5.95

LET'S KEEP MOVING — *Pete Snyder.* Travel with Peter to Haiti where he struggles with the call of God to be a missionary. Identify with Peter's growth of faith through trials and tribulations as he travels on to China where new adventures await and a kind endurance is needed ....#115-71 $9.95

RULING IN THEIR MIDST — *June Lewis.* The Lord has called us to rule even in the midst of all demonic activity and Satan's plans and schemes. Sister June has learned spiritual warfare from the Lord Himself, "who teacheth my hands to war," in the face of personal tragedy ....#108-73 $6.00

THE EYE OF THE NEEDLE — *Charlotte Baker.* These heavily anointed, life-changing prophetic parables will be used of the Holy Spirit to touch the depths of you and minister to your greatest needs ....#113-22 $3.00

Ad 6

THE GOLDEN AGE OF RETIREMENT — *Gen Siewiorek*. With humor and spiritual insight the author welcomes you to the world of retirement homes. She examines such sensitive and painful issues as losing one's independence, adjusting to the food and activities of retirement home living and facing what it means to grow old and eventually die .....#G400-68 $10.95

THE STORY OF THE GLORY — *Robert Doorn*. The Glory of God has followed Drs. Robert and Glenyce Doorn throughout their fifty years of ministry. You will be blessed as you witness almost every great move of God through their eye ....#118-77 $9.95

WESLEY'S SERMONS — *John Wesley*. Five sermons by this great saint whose love and compassion for souls helped produce the Great Awakening ....#107-00 $4.50

BOOKS RECOMMENDED BY ENGELTAL PRESS

AWAKENED BY AN ANGEL — *Carl W. Hahn, Jr*. Read the daily and nightly accounts of a retired denominational pastor who has been seeing light forms of angels and recording his experiences ever since ....#A400-26 $12.00

EDITED BY AN ANGEL — *Carl W. Hahn, Jr*. The continuing saga of Rev. Hahn's experiences as his Guardian Angel Precious assists in editing his book from his daily and nightly visitations ....#E400-030 $12.00

EVIDENCES OF THE FOOTPRINTS OF GOD— *Tommy Schmidt*. You will be thrilled with some of the wonderful facts and truths of the science of creation and the mysteries of the creative works of God ....#E118-69 $15.00

OH THAT ISHMAEL MIGHT LIVE — *Gene Little*. Through the author's love for the Muslim people which grew out of his journeys to the nations of this world, learn to overcome your fears and ignorance and bring life to Abraham's forgotten sons and daughters ....#O116-56 $15.00

TO LOVE A STRANGER — *Gene Little*. A biblical study introducing you to the blessings of hospitality and honors given to a Christian through the ministry of an open heart and open door ....#T113-11 $5.00

WELLSPRING OF WISDOM — *Gene Little*. The stories Jesus told centuries ago are as fresh today as they were two thousand years ago. Each generation has tried to catch these truths and insights. Be renewed in your faith and refreshed in the Spirit of Jesus through His parables ....#W300-38 $15.00

BOOKS ABOUT HEAVEN

INTRA MUROS — *Rebecca Springer*. One of the most beautiful books about Heaven available in its unabridged form. Read the glorious account of this ordinary believer's visit to Heaven ....#103-19 $8.00

PARADISE, THE HOLY CITY AND TH GLORY OF THE THRONE — *Elwood Scott*. Visited by a saint of God who spent forty days in Heaven, Elwood Scott's detailed description will edify and comfort your heart. Especially good for those with lost loved ones ....#104-97 $8.00

CHILDREN'S BOOKS

LITTLE ONES TO HIM BELONG—*Gwen Shaw*. Based on the testimonies of children's visions of Heaven and the death of a small Chinese boy, Sister Gwen weaves a delightful story of the precious joys of Heaven for children of all ages ....#103-88 $9.00

TELL ME THE STORIES OF JESUS—*Gwen Shaw*. Sister Gwen takes some of the greatest New Testament Stories of the Life of Jesus and writes them in a way that will interest children and help them to love Jesus........#106-37 $9.00

PROPHECIES AND VISIONS

THE DAY OF THE LORD IS NEAR: Vol. I - IV—*Engeltal Press*. "Surely the Lord GOD will do nothing, but he revealeth his secret unto his servants the prophets." (Amos 3: 7) A collection of prophecies, visions and dreams. This startling compilation will help you understand what God has in His heart for the near future ....$10.00 each
....Volumes I - IVwith binder-10#119-99 $25.00